Dr. Kim Gil-Youn (Grace Kim)

She was born on February 18, 1952 in Yeoui-ri Yonghwa-myeon,
Yeongdong County in Chungbuk Province of South Korea. She graduated from Chungbuk Youngdong Women's High School. She received a bachelor's degree in Korean Language and Literature from International University of Korea, a master of arts and a Ph.D. degree from Seokyeong University.
She is the chairman of DongJack Foundation for Arts and Culture, the president of Dongjack branch of Korean Writers Association, an advisory committee member of Korea-US Alliance Foundation, and the chairperson of Yeongdong County Residents Association in Seoul.

She runs a beautiful cafe, Crazer Coffee & Lounge near Gwangneung Arboretum, where cultural scents and music flow, and paintings with poems and artworks are displayed.

She is a visiting professor in the department of the Faculty of Arts of Seokyeong University, a member of the Board of Unification Education of the South Korean Ministry of Unification, a member of the National Unification Advisory Council, governor of the Institute for National Business Strategy, and the president of PTPI Korea Headquarters. She won the Presidential Award in 2006 for her contribution to the development of national unification, the Sinzisikin (New Knowledge Worker of Korea) Award for her contribution to future planning as the best individual who brought glory to Korea in 2013, and the Korean Filial Piety Grand Award in 2015, 2019 8A's Distinguished ROK Civic Leader Award.

She is a member of the Korean Writers Association and the PEN Korea and a director of the Korea Essayists Association. She served as the president of the New Korea Literary Society, the vice president of Sowol Memorial Society, and the president of Songpa Essayists Society. She won the Korea Writers Award in 2008, the New Korea Literature Award and the Tammi Literature Award in 2009, and the Sejong Literature Award in 2013. Her literary works are collection of essays, *In the Rising Mist*, an opera script, *Ttunabawi*, and so on. She has two children one is a professor at a medical school and the other is a pharmacist in the United States, she is now doing art and working to develop the Korean culture with her husband, who is a pharmacist and the writer of the novel, *Ttunabawi*.

사랑은 흐른다

김길연 시집

Love Goes By

Grace Kim

서문 Preface

봄날

아득히 먼 길을 달려 왔습니다.
지금은 뒤돌아 보아도 보이지 않는
다시 가려해도 가볼 수 없는
내 인생의 봄은 그렇게 흔적도 없이
가버렸습니다.
보릿고개 숨차게 달려 넘었던
첩첩산중 노랗던 고향의 봄
긴긴해 산마루 넘을까 마주 달리면
등 뒤에서 딸랑이던 양은 도시락
허기진 봄 길을 걷고 또 걸었습니다.
황토 빛 대지 위에 푸른 바람 불고
꽃구름 피어나는 황홀한 봄날
아버지 지게 위에 꽂힌 진달래
흰나비 노랑나비 춤추며 논둑길 가고
한줌 봄바람에 설레이는 수양버들
더 넓은 세상으로 달려가고만 싶어
수줍게 기다리던 소녀의 분홍빛 마음
불타오른 사랑으로 복사꽃이 피었습니다
질마재 넘어 저 멀리 저녁놀 가에
아련히 피어오르던 밥 짓는 연기
보고 싶은 내 어릴 적 거울
깊은 우물 속에 잠겨 있고
하늘처럼 열린 내 마음 파도가 출렁일 때
지상으로 낙하하는 꽃 그림자 따라
또 한 해의 봄이 떠나갑니다
더 넓은 세상에서
청춘도 사랑도 한때 왕성하였다
푸른 하늘에서 희망을 찾고
반짝이는 별에서 행복을 찾아
이 세상 이을 아이들도 키우고
후회 없는 생애 만드는데 정성도 기울였네
자신에게 부끄럽지 않은 사람이 되자던
나와의 약속
이제는 마무리 잘하는 것이
내게 남은 마지막 소임이라네
아름다운 세상 아름다운 인생
진정 나는 잘살고 있는 것인가?

2015. 11.
김길연

I have been too far away:
The spring days of my life disappeared
Without a trace
And I cannot go back to those days.
Spring dropped in yellow color
At my hometown in the heart of the mountains;
I endured the period of spring poverty
Hearing the clattering of
My empty nickel-silver lunchbox on my back
While running along the ridges
To get home before dark.
On a beautiful spring day
When the azure breeze stroked the red land
And fleecy clouds floated in the sky,
My father went along the bank between rice fields,
Carrying an A-frame on his back,
On which a bunch of azaleas had been put.
I was happy to follow him
With the white and yellow butterflies.
Weeping willows fluttered
In the spring breeze,
The girl's heart wanted to go into the wide world
Fired like a peach blossom.
Smoke from cooking rice went up
In the evening glow
Over Zilmajae Hill,
The girl's mind was rolling like waves
Deep in the well of my mirror.

The spring of life leaves again
With falling flowers.
In a wider world
My love and youth were full of vigor.
I looked for hope in the blue sky
And happiness from the shining stars.
I did my best to nurture my children
Who would inherit this world,
And for my life to be without regrets.
I promised myself
I would never bring shame to me.
And now, my ultimate responsibility is
To sail off into the sunset.
It is beautiful life and a beautiful world!
Am I leading a true life in that world?

번역: 라이채
덕성여대 영어영문과 졸업, 현재 번역작가로 활동 중이며, 다수의 영한 한영 번역서가 있다.

사진: 이동훈
부산외대 졸업, 스톡사진 작가로 활동 중이다.

캘리그라피: 허욱 강남대학교 교수

목차 Contents

그리움 *Longing*

봄바람 *Spring Wind*

강물 *The River*

사랑 *Love*

인생 *Life*

그리움

Longing

사랑은 흐른다 ①

그리움

어젯밤 꿈속에서 보았네
산그림자 안고 도는 정다운 오솔길

눈을 감고 찾아가는 마음의 고향
꿈속에서 찾아가는 그리운 그곳

천년이어 변함없는 기나긴 강물
풀벌레 합창하면 떠오르던 달

우물가 두레박은 허공에 걸려있고
별빛도 외로워 혼자 서산을 넘네
돌담길 돌아들면 환히 웃던 그 님은
지금은 어디론가 사라져 버리셨네

아련히 떠오르는 그리운 사람
그 얼굴 그리워 눈물지었네

언젠가 만나리라 그리운 이들
눈을 감고 찾아가는 마음의 고향

Longing

Last night in my dream
I walked along the roundabout path
Of my dear hometown,
Holding to the shadow of the mountain.

The sights in my heart move me to tears:
The lazy long river that has flowed for thousands of years,
The moon rising to the sound of bugs,
The old faces of loved ones…

Now a bucket is hanging in the air over the well,
A lonely star goes over the western mountain,
And my love has gone away, he who used to greet me
With a bright smile over the stone wall.

I have a dream that I will meet my dear ones
There someday.

산 들 강 꽃 소녀

물 첩첩 산 첩첩 넓은 들 좁다란 강가
언덕에 조그만 초가집

가슴속에 품고 사는 일곱 빛깔 무지개
그것은 우리가 살아가는 의미라네
우물 안 개구리가 넓은 세상 꿈꾸며
오늘이 힘들어도 계속 헤엄을 치는 이유
그것은 파란 불꽃 일으키는 존재의 이유

창공으로 솟구치는 종달새처럼
기쁨 넘치는 환희의 탄성
끝없이 사랑하고 신뢰하는 그 님을 만나
이 험한 세상을 살 만한 곳이라 위안케 하니
좁은 문 향하여 두려움 없이 발걸음 옮기고

강바람 푸른 초원
밤하늘 수많은 별들
반짝이는 눈동자 해맑은 두 눈
탐스럽게 피어나는 사계절의 꽃
산과 들 강 따라 피어난 꽃
그 이름은 산 들 강 꽃 소녀라네

푸른 안개 헤치고 반짝이는 태양
아래 피어나는 꽃 소녀라네
깊은 산 향하여 가슴을 열고
생전 처음 산 올라 기차 구경
설레던 꽃 소녀 소원은 하나
세상 사람 가슴속에 꽃 한 송이 피우리라
세상 사람 가슴속에 꽃 한 송이 피우리라

Mountain, Field, River, Flower, and a Girl

At a tiny thatch-roofed house on a low hill
In the middle of a large field
By a small river surrounded mountains.

A girl kept on swimming.
She was dreaming of the wide world,
Cherishing rainbow-colored hopes
With a flame of her sense of existence.

When meeting a descent person
She could love and trust,
The girl was in raptures of happiness,
Becoming like a lark soaring in the air,
Being comforted regarding living
In this troubled world,
And she walked toward the narrow gate fearlessly.

A girl with twinkling bright eyes
Was reared by things in nature
Such as the breeze from the river,
Millions of stars in the night sky,
And the charming flowers blooming
Along the way to the fields and mountains.

Like the sun breaking through the fog,
The girl, ascended the mountain
And saw a running train
For the first time in her life,
And came out as a flower.
She wished to bloom like a flower
In people's minds.

고향

말없이 산 중턱에 올라 당신을 봅니다
내 얼굴 내가 볼 수 없어 거울을 보듯
셀 수 없는 시간 한 자세로 기다린
당신 모습에서 어머니를 봅니다

솔바람 싱싱했던 그때 그 황홀함
내 푸르렀던 젊은 날의 모습
당신이 더 많이 간직하고 있지요
긴 그리움으로 침묵하며 기도하는 당신
본 듯 만 듯 지나친 세월 너무도 길었습니다

먼 산 아지랑이 칼바람 잠재우고
송홧가루 노랗게 흩날리던 날
길을 찾아 떠난 미지의 세계에서
천둥번개 몰아치고 세찬 소나기 한가운데
속절없이 서 있을 때도
당신은 언제나 제 곁에 있었습니다

크고 넓은 치마폭에 새 생명을 감싸 안고
푸른 빛 살며시 감추고 침묵으로 다독일 때
당신의 가이없는 염원은 무지갯빛으로
바람도 되고 물도 되고 길도 되었습니다

어디서나 그리워했던 어머니 품속
언덕 넘어 구부러진 길 산모퉁이 돌아
흐르는 물처럼 지나간 추억 노래하는
여기에 서서 따스한 당신 마음 들여다봅니다

이제
멀고먼 우주 돌아 지구로 회귀하는
한낱 티끌로 기나긴 여정
외로운 나그네 방랑을 접으니
가슴속에 숨어만 있던 하얀 바람이
파아란 환희로 휘파람을 불어봅니다

My Home

At halfway up the mountain
I am looking down at you silently;
It is as if I'm looking at myself in the mirror.
You remind me of my mother
Who constantly waited for me.

You treasured my younger days
That were full of fresh, green air,
And thrills.
However, for many years,
I was indifferent to you
Who had silently prayed for me.

Even when I got caught in a rainstorm,
After I left you to find a new world,
When the spring haze calmed down the cold wind
And pine pollens were flying
You still stood by me.

Putting your new ambitions aside,
You wrapped a new life in your large skirt
And stroked her tenderly,
Your grandiose desires toward her
Became the wind, the water, and the way.

Wherever I was,
How much I missed you
Seemingly like a mother's bosom.
After turning the corner of the winding hills,
Now I am here by the stream,
That is flowing along singing my old memories,
As I try to look into your warm heart.

After finishing the wandering of a lonely traveler
Running through the distant universe,
Now I get back to earth as merely dust,
The white wind has held a place in my heart
As it joyfully blows a blue whistle.

나의 역사

알 수 없는 먼 우주공간을 이름 모를 별로 떠돌다가
진주처럼 빛나는 영혼을 안고
햇살 눈 부신 땅으로 살며시 내려앉았네

인적 드문 깊은 산골 봄바람 불어오고
긴 돌담 돌아들면 황토 빛 고요한 초가집
아롱다롱 옹기종기 숨결을 나누며 키가 자라고
자애로운 사랑 속에 눈망울 반짝이며 꿈을 꾸었네

푸르른 청보리 밭이랑을 닮아
언제나 정갈하고 어여쁘던 어머니
흔들리는 호롱불 아래 검정고무신 기우시고
보리개떡 쑥버무리 나물죽에 고구마도
사랑 많은 당신 있어 든든했지요

영롱한 새벽이슬 떨치고 굽이굽이 산길 따라
숨 차오르던 30리 등하교길
진달래 삐꾸기 달래 냉이 철 따라 함께 하던 길
두 발로 바람 가르며 세상과 마주 설 희망을 키웠습니다

산들이 겹겹이 싸여 하늘만 동그란 곳
그림처럼 아름다운 조그만 산골학교
졸업생이라야 모두가 열여덟 명
모두가 포기한 진학의 꿈 오직 혼자 갈고 닦았네

담임선생님 온종일 애태우며 시험 보는
단 한 명의 제자를 기다리시고
합격 소식 전하러 단숨에 달려간 20리길
저녁밥 짓느라 연기 자욱한 부엌에서 뛰어나오신 선생님
조그만 제자를 덥석 안고 마당을 빙빙 도니
푸른 하늘도 흰 구름도 부챗살처럼 퍼지며 같이 돕니다

My History

After floating through unknown space
Around the universe faraway,
I eventually landed on a sunny spot on earth
With a pearly bright soul.

In a secluded mountain valley
Through which a gentle spring breeze brushed past,
At a small thatch-roofed and red clayed cottage
Beyond a stone wall
I grew, feeling warmth
Among people huddled together.
I had dreams with my eyes twinkling,
Winning all hearts.

I had a mother who was always graceful and neat
Like the rows of the green barley field.
Even in black rubber shoes mended by her
Under the flickering kerosene lamp,
With poor meals like barley Gaetteok,
Wild green gruel, or sweet potatoes,
I felt I had a full stomach
Because of my mother's long-lasting love.

While walking the 30-ri round trip to school,
Brushing the pearls of early morning dew

Along the winding mountain path,
Where cuckoos, azaleas, wild chive, and shepherd's purses
Made the scenery change from season to season,
I nursed a hope to go out into the world
And to stand grandly dividing wind.

With a round sky in the heart of the mountains,
At a pretty and small school
That just had 18 graduates-to-be,
I prepared hard to go on to school,
While other friends hardly thought it possible
To go to upper school.

There was my homeroom teacher
Who waited with impatience while her only student
Took the entrance exam.
I rushed to her, a distance of 10-ri
With the letter of acceptance.
She came out from the smoky kitchen where rice was boiling
And hugged her little student
As she turned round and round in the yard
Making the clouds in the sky also circle
Like the spreading of a folded fan.

꽃의 소망

먼 하늘 잿빛구름
바람 재우면
산허리 아지랑이
춘설 여의고
잎도 없이 피어나는
두견새 울음

인적 드문 산모퉁이
소롯이 피어
붉디붉은 꽃잎새에
소망을 담고
하염없이 기다리는
두견의 마음

눈부신 햇살 아래
휘어 돌은 황톳길
철없이 조잘대는
눈 맑은 소녀

아버지 나뭇짐에
꽂힌 두견화
찬란한 봄이랑
나비랑 간다

A Flower's Wish

As the gray clouds moved off to a distance
The wind subsided,
And the spring snow thawed on the hillside,
The air shimmers,
The azaleas come out with no leaves
Like the cuckoo's sad song.

At an almost deserted corner
Of the mountain foot,
They waited long,
Including their hopes
In their very red petals.

In bright sunshine,
Turning around the corner
Of the red clay road,
The bright-eyed girl rattles on innocently.

The stack of wood
Decorated with azaleas,
Is loaded on the A-Frame
On the back of my father;
A butterfly goes after the flowers,
The glorious spring is going.

옛 그림자

내 기억력이 한계선에
넘치지 않았을 때

내 주위 아름다운 모든 것 모든 사람
아무리 그래도 거짓은 아니었다

출렁이는 물동이 이고 가는 긴 그림자
진달래 꽂힌 나뭇단 짊어진 뒷모양새
아랫집 아저씨 윗담의 춘자 엄마

후칭이 써레 빌려주고 빌려갈 때
서로 고개 한번 끄덕이면
차용증 영수증이 되었다

그런데
세상에 대고 거짓말 한 번 할 때마다
진실은 아프고
기억 속 순수는 하나씩 없어져 갔다

그래서 세상은 거짓말로
넘치고 넘치고 넘쳐서

세상이 거짓인지
내가 어쩜 거짓인지도 몰라
황망히 거울을 보면

거기 또 거짓으로 표정 지은
또 다른 내가 남아
온전한 옛날의 나를 그리워하고 있다

The Old Shadow

When I was not mentally overloaded,
There were no cheaters around me,
There were only beautiful surroundings.

Chunja's mom's long shadow,
Who lived upstairs,
Carrying a water jar on her head.
An uncle living downstairs,
Carrying a bundle of firewood
With azaleas in it on his back.

When Huching nodded his head,
When borrowing a harrow from my house,
It played the role of a receipt.

And afterwards,
Whenever I told a lie to the world,
The truth was distorted,
Purity in my memory was damaged
Little by little
Until the world was flooded with lies.

Sometimes I looked into the mirror,
Being confused.
Was the world false or me?
There was another me
Who makes a false statement,
Yet longing for the time before purity passed.

젊은 날의 꿈

꿈! 그것은 희망으로 가는 징검다리였네
사방이 막혀 하늘만 동그랗게 보이는 첩첩산중에서
그때 더 넓은 세상으로 비상하는 꿈을 꾸지 않았다면
지금은 어디에서 무엇이 되어 무엇을 하고 있을까?

깊은 산속으로 소풍 간 어느 날
높은 산을 오르면 기적소리가 들린다고
악착같이 작은 몸으로 산을 오르던 조그만 소녀
아무리 기다려도 기차를 볼 수 없었던 소녀
멀리에서 희미한 기적소리와 뿌연 연기만 보았네

네잎클로버를 찾아 행운을 점치던 작은 소녀
삼년 동안 하루도 거르지 않고 교무실에 꽃을 꽂던 꿈
언젠가 세상에 예쁜 꽃을 활짝 피우리라 다짐하던 꿈

시작이 한발 늦었으니 가는 길도 더디다
서른일곱 늦깎이 대학생 두 아이와 같이 학생
아이도 시험이면 엄마도 시험
학부형에 학생 노릇 그래도 행복한 인생이라네

Dream of Youth

A dream was a stepping-stone that led me to hope;
If I had not dreamed of flight toward the wider world,
But had rested on, living deep in the mountain
Just seeing the round sky,
I wonder where I would be and what I would be doing now.

I was a tiny girl who tried hard to climb a high mountain,
Having convinced myself
That I would be able to see a train passing by,
But I just heard the sound of its whistle
And saw the smoke puffed out of it
After the train had departed.

I was a little girl who would look for four-leaf clovers
Which are a token of good luck;
I was a girl who put flowers in a vase
In the teacher's room every day for three years
Dreaming of blooming beautiful flowers
That would someday fill the world.

As I fell a step behind, I am slow in progress;
I am a college student at 27, and am like my two children;
Even as a busy student and a parent,
Life is still wonderful.

온고이지신 溫故以知新

가신님 길 따라 걸어봅니다
아득히 머-언
옛 님 살았던 그때 그 시간

오천 년 전 오백 년 전
옛 님 마음 엿보며
가신님 길 따라 걸어봅니다

님들의 사색 님들의 사랑
흰 종이 검은 먹물 속에
면면히 살아 있어

그때가 오늘인 양
가신님 발자취 따라
오늘도 걸어봅니다

Reviewing the Old and Learning the New

I try to follow the way
You, our ancestors went down;
I try to go back to the time you lived.

Following the way,
I try to look into your hearts,
What you would have felt 500 or 5,000 years ago.

Your thoughts, your love…
They still live on the white paper
And in the brush writings in black.

I try to follow the way
You walked,
Regarding that day as today.

산사의 念

너무 고요해 잠들지 못하고
너무 멀어 잊지 못하는

잎 새 하나 없이 더 푸르르고
좁디좁아 더 넓은 곳

끝없이 출렁이는 생명의 가지 끝

바람이 바위 끝을 스치듯 스치듯
강물이 산자락을 감돌 듯 감돌 듯

너무 높아 푸른 하늘
너무 높아 검은 우주

한점 바람으로
한점 티끌로
가이 없이 날고 싶어라

Thoughts in a Temple

The night is too quiet to sleep,
My love is too far away to forget.

The mountain is dark green
Showing no leaves.
My room is tiny but an open field.

The night is full of vitality.

Wind plays on the rocks,
The river water hangs over
The foot of the mountain.

The high sky looked blue,
The immense universe looked black.

I would like to fly there
As a mote
That is free as the wind.

축복의 섬 코와이

역사도 알 수 없는 푸른 섬들이
바다 가운데서 점으로 숨 쉬고
코발트빛 물과 하늘이 구름으로 만나는 곳

코끼리 닮아 순하게 누워있는 코와이 섬 섬 섬

흐르는 세월이 노랫가락 읊조리는 물결사이 머물고
형형색색 산호들이 꿈을 먹고 자라는 곳
이곳이 푸른 바다 평화세상 코와이라네

섭리의 어버이 품에 안겨 숨어 피는 산호들의 합창
그들의 노랫소리 높이 들리면
깊은 마음 한 점 바다에 넣어
평화세상 이루려 사랑 담는 이
이들 있어 코와이 섬은
영적 세계 열어 줄 낙원으로 바뀌어 간다

淸海 맑은 바다 깊은 물에 평화를 심는
박애정신 크고 맑은 병화와 정해가 있더라
하늘의 섭리 살아 숨 쉬는 이곳 그 증거가 되리라

The Blessed Island, Kowhai

Despite having no acceptable histories,
The green dot-like islands are full of life
In the middle of the sea,
Where the cobaltic water and sky meet
Under the clouds.

The island, island, island...
Lying modestly like an elephant.

The years flowing by break over the waves,
The colorful coral grows up with dreams,
Here in the peaceful sea world, Kowhai!

There are some people
Who try with all their hearts to change the island
To a spiritual and peaceful paradise,
While listening to the chorus of the coral,
Blooming in the arms of providence,

The heroes are Byeong-hwa and Jeong-hae
With a benevolent spirit and a fresh mind,
Who instill peace in the depths of the clean sea.

봄바람

Spring Wind

사랑은 흐른다 ②

봄바람

그을음의 계절 봄바람은
수줍은 여인의 볼우물을 더 깊게 파고

꽃바람의 계절 봄바람은
물오른 여인의 치마폭을 더 세게 흔드네

누가 부르는가
시냇물 청량한
대자연의 노래를

누가 부르는가
솔바람 향기 담은
사랑의 노래를

새봄 오는 소리
귀 끝에 담고
흰 눈 살던 곳에
나들이 가면

지난겨울 밟고 간
내 발자국
어디론가 사라지고

또다시 만드는
내 역사는
오늘도 맨땅에서
헤엄을 치네

언제 미소 지은 얼굴로
내 눈을 마주하고 마음을 쓰다듬으랴
또 들여다봐도 또 비어 있는
나의 우물은 그 언제나 채워지랴

갈 길 멀어 허허로운 들판에
마음만 다급하여
여덟 길 다 가고픈 나의 마음이
오늘도 봄바람 따라 줄달음친다

Spring Wind

The spring wind, tanning the skin,
Makes the shy ladies' dimples deeper;

The spring wind, producing flowers,
Flutters the blooming girls' skirts stronger.

Who can sing the song of Mother Nature,
Clear and cool like the murmur of a stream?

Who can sing the song of love,
Fragrant like the pine scent
Wafted in on the wind?

With the spring coming in my ears,
I go on a picnic to the snow land

And find none of the footprints
I made last winter in the snow,

I try to make myself another history
On bare ground.

When can I console my heart
With smiling eyes?
When can my empty well be filled
Quickly enough to satisfy me?

Standing in the empty field of life,
My heart that wants to go on eight roads,
Runs, dividing the spring wind
Because they are long ways for me to go.

봄의 향기

푸른 들판
가로질러 달리는 버스
파밭이랑 상추랑 미나리꽝도
장화 신은 아저씨 고무 다라이로 배 띄우고
한 줌 한 줌 쓱 쓱 미나리 향기를 베네

꽃내음 풀내음 미나리내음
색색 가지 내음이 찻길로 나와
달려가는 버스에 부서질수록
더 멀리 퍼져 가는 들녘의 향기

Scents of Spring

Through the window of the bus,
Running across the green field,
The patches of green onions, lettuce,
And water parsley flash fast.
A man wearing boots cuts water parsley plants
With their scent and puts them into a container
Afloat like a ship.

The scents of flowers, green grass,
And water parsley break
Over the bow of the bus
Spread far away.

봄의 노래

별빛 담고 달빛 담아
겨울을 열고
봄바람 꽃바람
봄을 열었네

하아얀 분홍으로
꽃잎을 담고
푸른빛 앞치마를
잊지 않았네

지난가을
낙엽을 목에 두르고
이른 봄
노래로 잠을 깨우는
고향집 앞마당
복사꽃 나무

파란 향기 노란 향기
봄 향기 안에
눈감으면 떠오르는
황홀한 사랑

Song of Spring

After spending winter
By moonlight and starlight
A gentle breeze opens spring.

Spring wore a lime-green apron
And put white and pink petals
In the front pocket of the apron.

In the front yard of my old home
The peach tree, wearing necklece
Of the fallen leaves of last autumn,
Awakens from its sleep
By the spring songs.

Being lost in the blue
And yellow scents of spring,
I close my eyes
To meet my charming love.

오월 들녘

세모 네모 물 가두고 못자리 보는
종아리에 거머리 없는 신식 농부는

쇠스랑 써레질은 하지도 않고
소 몰고 논두렁도 다니지 않네

닭장같이 포개놓은 아파트 안고
마지못해 누워있는 앉은뱅이 산

발밑에 흐르는 가재 없는 개울은
네모 세모 논배미에 물을 채워서
물방개 소금쟁이 고울고울 헤엄치게 해놓고

구불구불 요리조리 반짝반짝 방개처럼
논두렁 헤엄쳐 가는 씨앗 없는 농부들

어디에 무엇으로 농사를 지으려
엔진 소리 신나게 논두렁 생긴 대로
요리조리 쉴 새 없이 달려나가나

The Field of May

A modern farmer,
With no leech clinging to his leg,
Is preparing a rice seed plot
By filling squares and triangles with water.

He doesn't need any pitchfork or harrow
To level the ground,
Or any cow to pull a plough.

The platform hills lie
Holding the apartment complexes reluctantly,
On which many houses are stacked up
Like chicken houses.

They made a nice stream,
But there is no crawfish.
They made a strip of a paddy field,
Where there are some diving beetles
And pond skaters swimming.

The farmer is busy walking
Along the winding ridges,
But he has no seeds.

How come he just runs along the path
With a purring engine,
Not knowing how or what to do
For farming?

오월의 노래

아카시아의 향기에 취해 오월을 사노라
청보리밭 길 걸으며 오월을 사노라
푸르른 산하 가슴에 담으며 오월을 사노라

그 옛날 파란 꿈 이루려 넘던 고갯길
이제는 저 멀리 있고
청운의 산봉우리 머리에 이고
환희에 떨었던 날들도
이제는 저 멀리 있네

내 삶의 오솔길 굽이굽이 돌아
지금 서 있는 곳 어디쯤일까
아름다웠던 사랑
잊지 못할 그날들
이제는 모두가 그리운 사람들

바람 부는 언덕에 서서
아카시아 향기에 취해 오월을 사노라
청보리밭 길 걸으며 오월을 사노라
푸르른 산하 가슴에 담으며 오월을 사노라

May Song

In May
I live lost in the fragrance of acacia blossoms,
Walking along the field of green barley,
Keeping green nature next to my heart.

The hill which I went over
With my young dreams and
The days when I was overwhelmed with joy
On the peak that offered my young aspirations,
Is now far away.

Winding around the trail of life,
Where am I now?
The beautiful love,
The unforgettable days,
Where are they now?

On the windy hill of May,
I am lost in the fragrance of acacia blossoms,
Walking along the field of green barley,
While keeping green nature to my heart.

오월의 창가

5월
창가가 푸르르다
모진 추위 무거운 흙 견디고
너도나도 싹 틔운 눈 들이
잎으로 피어나 웃고 있다

때로는 꽃으로
때로는 향기로
또 한 해 살아 낼
용기를 채우려
바람에도 비에도
지지 않으려 애쓰고 있다

멀리서 가까이서
보이는 푸르름
물 한 모금
햇살 하나에도
몸부림치며
만들어 낸 풀색들이 모여

오월의 창가를
그토록 푸르게 푸르게
만들고 있다

May Window

In May,
The windows are green;
Through the windows,
Buds are smiling,
Having survived the bitter cold
And broken through the thick earth.

They are trying to build up strength
To live the year,
Protecting themselves,
Their flowers,
And their fragrance
From the wind and the rain.

The green color,
Close and far,
That was concentrated
Even in a drop of water
And a beam of sunlight;

So it makes the May windows
Green and green.

별내면 들녘

별내면 들녘은
별들의 잔치

하늘에서 반짝이던
은하수 쏟아져 내려

별내면 들녘은
하이얀 별들로 뒤덮여 버렸다

전설의 바다에 눈이 내린 듯
끝없이 펼쳐진 배꽃의 향연

눈부신 꽃향기에 취해버린 여심은
오지도 않을 백마 탄 왕자를 기다리고

별내면 들녘은 별들의 잔치
가도 가도 눈부신 배꽃의 향연
가도 가도 눈부신 배꽃의 향기

The Field of Star Stream Town

The party of stars is in full swing
In the field of Star Stream Town.

The stars twinkling in the galaxy
Came pouring down here.

The field of Star Stream Town
Is covered with the shiny stars.

It is a great feast of pear blossoms
Across the endless field,
Like a snow covered legendary sea.

Lost in the fragrance of blossoms,
A woman's heart is waiting for Prince Charming
Who will never come.

Stars throw a party in the field of Star Stream Town;
It is a feast of the pear blossoms,
Dazzling white endlessly.

아침 산

이른 봄엔
알몸 다 드러내놓고
해바라기 봄바라기
비바라기 하던

산모퉁이 휘감으며
눠어진 산길
도란도란 정겨웁고

어느 날 문득
綠陰으로 앞을 가리고
鄕愁에 젖은
눈 속으로 들어와 앉네

수줍은 듯 살며시
안개를 포옹하고
새벽이슬 덧이불로
늦잠을 자다

짙푸른 녹음으로
화장을 하고
살랑이는 산들바람
희롱에 치마를 드는
근엄한 듯 새침 떠는
초여름 아침 산

Morning Mountain

In the early spring
How it desired sunlight and rain
Showing its naked body!

The sight of the winding roads
Along the mountainside
Rouses a feeling of warmth.

Before I know it
It has rushed vegetation
To paint my eyes with green
And make me sick for home.

It gets up late
Hugging fog maiden-like, gently
Covered with the early morning dew
As its blanket.

Now in early summer
The morning mountain,
Adorns itself in green,
Pulls up its leaf skirt
Attracted by the breeze
Seemingly prim and proper.

初夏

초록 초록
초록바다
푸른 푸른
푸른바다

오월은 오월은
푸르른 바다

싱그러운 파란 바람
앞서 달리면
키자란 보리바람
뒤를 따른다

뒷동산 솔바람
말을 달리면
산하에 일렁이는
푸르른 파도

앞뜨락 뒷뜨락
동구 밖에도
라일락 아카시아
찔레꽃 속에

향기로운 꽃내음
가득 찼어라
오월은 오월은
향그런 바다

Early Summer

Blue, blue,
Blue sea.
Green, green,
Green sea.

May,
May is a green sea.

The refreshing blue breeze
Runs first,
The green zephyr follows it,
Brushing the grown barley

A galloping horse dividing the breeze
Stroking pine leaves on the back hill,
The green waves are rolling
Through the fields and mountains.

In the front yard,
In the back yard,
And in the outskirts of the village
Are lilac, acacia, and wild roses in full bloom.

May,
May is a fragrant sea
Full of flower scents.

가을의 緖

지난여름이 있어
가을은 더 기품이 있고
아픔을 이긴 삶이
더욱 값지듯이

지난밤의 어둠은
아침을 더욱 밝게 하였고
여름날의 녹음은 붉은 꽃을
더욱 붉게 만들었네

이제 마지막 남은 햇살로
노란 꽃은 더 노랗게 하시고
마지막 핏빛 단풍으로
겨울의 흰 눈을 더욱 희게 만드소서

기도 속에 영글어가는 열매들에
단맛을 더욱 깊게 하시고
한겨울 배불리 먹을
영양을 채워주소서

줄지어 선 무궁화가
은근과 끈기를 보여 준다 하여도
벌레 많아 제대로 꽃을 피우지
못함도 기억하소서

시고 떫은 인생의 맛일지라도
우리의 생 한가운데 사랑의 탑이 자리하고

진솔한 삶으로 속을 채워
쏠쏠한 열매 거두는
부끄럽지 않은
모두의 가을 되게 하소서

Prelude to the Fall

Fall comes more gracefully
Because there was last summer
Where we had to bear the heat.

Like the morning dawns brighter
Because there was last night,
The lush green trees made flowers
More red.

May the remaining intense sunlight
Make yellowish flowers become deep yellow ones,
Maple leaves become blood-red ones
To make the snow be whiter beside it in the winter!

May fruits growing ripe
And add sweetness
To let us have our fill
Even in the midwinter!

Please remember the roses of Sharon,
An example of patience and placidity,
Though not having many flowers
Because of many bugs!

Though the taste of life is bitter and sour,
There is a tower of love in the middle of it.

Bless us to have an honorable
And fruitful fall
Filled with sincerity
And fidelity!

가을 단상

하느님이 보일 만치
맑은 하늘은
푸르른 마음으로
기도 올리게 하고

마음속 깊이 감춰진
잿빛 사랑을 불러올리네

세상살이 절반 넘은
여인 닮은 코스모스

무심한 듯 바람에 몸을 맡기고
몸을 꼬고 희롱하는 고추잠자리
얇고 붉은 입술에 키스를 하네

이무기가 떠나간 초가지붕엔
시집 못 가 수줍은
언니 닮은 하이얀 박꽃

전설처럼 피어나
가을밤을 수놓고 있네

Musing on Autumn

The sky is clear and high
Enough to see God.
It drives me to prayer
With a bright hope;

It evokes a faded love
In the bottom of my heart.

The cosmos looking like women
At the midstream of life;

The red dragonflies make themselves delightful
And kiss the red lips
That committed themselves to the wind,
With their whole bodies;

On the thatched roof
Where a python might have left
Snow-white gourd flowers smile shyly
Like my unmarried older sister;

They light the autumn night,
As if it is a scene from a legend.

가을 숲

내 창문 아래
눈으로 밟히는 낙엽바다에
나는 봄부터
가보고 싶어 안달했었다

흙냄새 담고
연초록 새잎이 피어날 때도
진달래 아카시아 밤꽃이
번갈아 피어날 때도

뜨거운 태양 아래
진초록 숲이 출렁일 때도
내 마음은 언제나
너에게로 달려갔었다

그때 나는
이미 보았었지
꽃보다 더 화려한
너의 마지막 불꽃을

아련하고 흐드러지고
쌉상한 너의 향기에선
하이얀 눈꽃냄새가 났었지

가지마다 피었던 꽃술에서
남겨진 새 생명이
남은 날들을 헤아리는 오늘

비로소 나는 너를 보고
하늘이 비어 있음을 안다

Autumn Woods

Over my window,
The sea of dead leaves,
Are crunched in the snow.
I would like to go to meet you even in spring.

I wanted to go to meet you
Even when the new leaves sprouted
Pervading the air with an earthy smell,
Or when the azaleas, acacia and chestnut blossoms
Bloom by turns.

When green waves are were rolling
Through the woods under the hot sun,
My heart always run to you.

I already knew that
Your last flame
Would be more gorgeous
Than any flowers.

I smell the scent of pure snow
From your pale
And splendid dryness.

A new life is left
On the stamen of every branch
To make count the day to come.

As I come to meet you today,
You remind me
That the sky is empty.

가을 풍경

빗겨 가는 햇살에
마음 졸이는
늦둥이 조롱박

발가벗고서
하늘 향해 내어 뻗은
더듬이 닮은
순하디순한
조롱박 잎새

달팽이 집을 지고
이사를 가듯
가냘픈 줄기에
조롱을 달고

여름부터 가을까지
기다려 왔네

하 많은 낮과 밤에
다시 도려낼
하이얗고 부드러운
속을 채우고

안으로 안으로
세월을 담아

물도 술도 초연해질
마음을 다지네

Autumn Scenery

A late baby-naked bottle gourd
Is anxious about whether
Sunshine will veer away.

The tender gourd vines
Creep up toward the sky,
As if they are antennae.

The slender vines hung by dippers
Are like small snails
Carrying one big shell.

To fill the inside,
Though that will be scraped out finally,
And fatten their white and soft skin,
They have survived
For many days and nights
Since last summer,

Including time
Into them,

Hardening their heart
To accommodate water, wine,
Or anything.

겨울 숲

꽤 벗은 아이 마냥 배꼽 내놓고
全裸로 시위하는 겨울 산 나목
모처럼 열린 백설의 향연
눈꽃으로 화안해진 얼굴을 들고

노루 토끼 발자국 소리 좇아
귀 기울이면
계곡에 갇혀 버린
바람소리 물소리가

옛날 얘기 같이하자 칭얼거리면
두 팔 흔들어 바쁘다고 대답할 때
먼 산 위 날고 있는 갈까마귀는
무엇을 귀 기울여 듣고 있을까

십 년을 한자리에 붙박혀 서서
세상소식 내음으로 다 안다네
때로는 향기롭고 때로는 악취이지만
그것이 세상사라네

두꺼운 눈 이불 속에
새봄의 향기 가득하고
어두운 흙더미 속에
새싹이 가득하듯
쌩한 바람 스쳐 가는 겨울 숲에는
하이얀 눈 이불 속에
아가가 새근새근 잠자고 있다

Winter Woods

Absolutely nude trees,
Exposing their navels
Like naked boys;
They enjoy a banquet of white snow,
Smiling a bright smile in the snow flowers.

When they listen to the sound of the footsteps
Of roe deer and rabbits,
The wind and water
Trapped in the valley whine to talk with them.

When the trees wave away,
Refusing the request of wind and water,
Ravens tilt their heads
Flying over the far away mountain.

Staying in the same place for over ten years,
The trees tell by smell how the world is;
Sometimes, it is aromatic,
Other times, it smells bad.
But they know that it is the world.

Under the thick snow blanket
Is the fragrance of new spring,
Under the ground
Are sprouts that will come out soon;
Even as the cold wind crosses it,
The winter forest is like the warm blanket
Under which babies are sleeping peacefully.

강물 *The River*

사랑은 흐른다 ③

강물

아득히 먼 길
때론 침묵하며
여울목에 머물고

미지의 세계
두려움으로 서성인다

뒤돌아보아도 보아도
물안개에 쌓인
긴 그리움
구도하는 순례자
하나의 염원
생명 잇는 설렘으로
푸른 산 황톳길 감아 돈다

The River

On a long journey
There are times to be silent,
Times to be hesitant
In the neck of the rapids,
Or times to be afraid
For the unknown world.

It is a long longing,
Wet fog-bound
Even looking back on it
Again and again;
It is a pilgrim seeking the truth;
It winds among the green mountains
Or the red clay roads
With only one overwhelming wish
To join the life line.

벚꽃

한때는 왜꽃이라
미움받던 꽃

꿀 없이 벌 나비도
치지 못하고

향 없이 색만으로
더 현란하네

꽃비 되어 흩날리는
잎새 사이로

선열들 만세 소리
아우성 되어

봄 하늘 맑고 높게
떠올려지네

하 많은 벚잎마다
열린 설움들

반세기 지난 오늘
못다 푼 사연

왜꽃이여

이 땅에 피어 있는 줄
너는 아는가

Cherry Blossoms

Once you were hated among Koreans
Because you're Japanese flowers.

You are not attracted
By bees and butterflies.

You are gorgeous with only color
Without aroma, though.

Deceased patriots' shouts of viva
Between swirling your petals.

The sound seems to resound
High into the clear spring air.

The numerous leaves seemingly are heavy
With clusters of sorrow.

Even after half a century,
Unsolved issues remain between two nations.

Oh, you, Japanese flower!

Do you know why
You have blossomed in this land?

장미의 아픔

찬란한
오월 햇살 아래
핏빛 꽃으로
피어난 아픔

짙푸른 잎새에
숨겨진 가시
그 뉘를
해코지 했으리오

서울 부산 광주에
넘치는 강물 되어
흐르는 크디큰 통곡

참으로 아름다운
생명의 향기
줄지어 피어난
선홍빛 희망

짙푸른 잎새에
가려진 가시
그 뉘를
해코지 하리오

The Pain of Rose

In brilliant May sunshine
It blooms blood-red pain.

Was there anyone who got hurt
By the thorns hidden
Behind the deep green leaves?

In Seoul, Busan, and Gwangju
The red roses make a red river
Flowing with a rush,
Crying their hearts out.

That is the fragrance
Of a beautiful life;
The scarlet hopes
That bloomed in a row.

Is there anyone who gets hurt
By the thorns hidden
Behind the deep green leaves?

국화꽃 향기

가을빛 빗겨 드는 삶의 창가에
한 송이 국화로 향기를 채워
어제 오늘 내일을 이으려 했네

바람에 흩날려간 젊음을 찾아
내일도 허공을 맴돌까

비 내리는 가을날엔
꽃잎이 한꺼번에 무너져 내려
영영 나를 찾지 못하고
더 멀리멀리 떠도는 향기

노을이 아름답게 찾아든 가을
푸르던 잎새들에
붉은 색깔로 나이를 새겨
세월이 흘렀음을 일러 주는가

뜨겁던 지난여름 혈기 왕성했었음은
이 가을의 준비였는가

쌉싸름한 가을내음
서리 위를 스칠 때
국화향보다 더 진한
인생의 향기 배어 나온다

Chrysanthemum Fragrance

Standing by the window
Bringing in autumn light,
I hope my life will always be filled
With a chrysanthemum fragrance
Yesterday, today, and tomorrow,
But not to float on the air
Longing for my younger days
That have gone, never to return.

On the rainy autumn days,
My heart collapsing like your petals falling,
I hover in mid-air like an aroma
Without getting myself together.

The autumn sky aglow
With the sunset,
The green leaves changing to red clothes,
Remind of the passing of time.
A passionate last summer
Was needed for autumn.
As the pungent essence of autumn
Brushes past frost,
Life smells thicker than a chrysanthemum.

눈꽃

봄에만 꽃이 피랴
겨울에 핀 꽃이
더없이 화려하다

아오모리 아키타
순백 천지에 늘어선 삼나무
때 묻어 얼룩진 세상
처음으로 되돌리는 너
난 분 분 하늘 뒤덮고
화려하게 춤추는 너
누구와 입맞춤하러 오는가

억겁의 인연으로
찾아낸 님이 있어
녹아드는 사랑으로
적막한 계곡 속에
바람으로 피는 꽃

살며시 품에 안겨
수줍은 눈꽃이여
영혼마저 잦아드는
황홀한 순간이여!

Snow Flowers

Flowers not only bloom in spring
But also in winter;
Winter flowers might be more beautiful.

On Aomori Akita,
The fringe of cedars
In the pure-white snowy field,
Over which snowflakes fly,
Dancing beautifully,
Looking for someone to kiss.
They erase tainted world
To return it to the beginning.

Finding lasting bonds,
They melt into their love
In a desolate valley
And finally come into snow flowers
At the mercy of the wind.

The snow flowers, nestling ashamedly
In their love's arms,
Are lost in delight;
Even their souls rest in peace!

들풀

햇살이 미소를 머금고
너의 등을 간지를 때

기-ㄴ 겨울잠에서
눈 비비고 일어나

기다릴 이 없는
세상으로 나가기 위해

보일 듯 말 듯
쬐그만 씨눈을 틔우고

봄이 물어다주는 단비와 바람을 먹고
너는 무연히 자란다

상처로 얼룩진 대지는
한없는 땜통을 너로 해서 때우고

우리는 잔인한 사월을 지나
푸르른 오월을 노래하며 너를 잊는다

실보다 가는 머리에 꽃을 피우고
밟혀도 베어도 불평 없는 너

황량한 세상을 초록으로 물들이고
희망이라 이름 지어

절망으로 살아가는 이들을
사랑으로 위로해 주네

Wild Grass

Wearing a smile
The sunshine tickles your back.

Rubbing your eyes,
You wake up from your long winter sleep,

Preparing yourself
To go out into the world
Where no one will welcome you.

Almost invisibly,
You germinate into a tiny bud,

And begin to grow night and day
In the spring rain with the fresh breeze.

You remove the stains of the earth
Made with wounds.

They forget you
While singing in the green May
After the cruelest month, April.

You make flowers on your stalk
As thin as a fine tread,
Never complaining when trampled
By animals and people.

You color the desolate world green,
In the name of Hope.

You comfort depressed people
And bring them love.

열매

열매의 어버이는
꽃이었습니다
아름답고 향기로운
꽃이었습니다
벌 나비 모여드는
꽃이었습니다

꽃의 어버이는
새싹이었습니다
삼라만상의 胎인
흙 속에서 꼬물꼬물
고귀한 생명을 모아
바람 이는 세상으로 올린

새싹의 어버이는
열매입니다
강한 지진에도
버틸 튼튼한 다리
어지러운 세상
포근히 감싸줄 잎새
우주보다 더 큰
꿈과 사랑을 키우는

그것은 바로 생명을
잉태한 열매입니다

Fruits

The parents of fruits
Were flowers,
Beautiful and fragrant,
Attracting bees and butterflies.

The parents of flowers
Were sprouts,
Going up into the windy world
Through the thick earth
That is the womb of all nature.

The parents of sprouts
Were fruits,
Having the potential for strong legs
Capable of sustaining them
Even in a strong earthquake,
For leaves are capable
Of wrapping the difficult world softly,
Having visions and dreams
Bigger than the universe.

It is a fruit that
Gives birth to a life.

빈 들판

너와 내가 하나 되어 흐르던 강이
무구한 시간 흘러 홀로되었다
어디서 무엇으로 너를 찾을꼬

천만년 꿈틀대는 地神의 광기
그것으로 싹 틔우고 열매를 맺어
너와 내가 지금까지 생명을 잇고

풍선같이 부풀은 세상 속에서
세포 속에 스며든 체액까지도
다 타버린 장작불같이
이제는 한 줌만큼도 남지 않았다

무엇으로 이 가슴을 가득 채워서
내 뒤 따를 이들에게
건네어 주랴
들판은 오늘도 점점 비어 가는데

Empty Field

The river that once ran
By you and me together as one
Ended up alone after many years.
Where and how can I find you?

By the earth god's ardent favor
For ten million years
We have carried on life
By budding and yielding fruits.

However,
Unlike the world swelled up like balloon,
Everything is dried up now,
Even cell sap,
Like the burnt-out wood pile.

What can I fill my empty heart with
To hand down to my offspring?
For the field becomes empty
More and more.

나무의 사색

끝없이 퍼져 가는 싱그런 화살
환희로 반짝이는 초록빛 향연

청명한 하늘이고 생각에 잠긴
역사의 꿈을 꾸는 아름드리 속

심연으로 가라앉듯 뻗어간 뿌리
돌돌돌 말아 올린 수액의 숨결

백 년을 한자리에 마음 모으고
동그란 나이테를 헤아려 간다

Trees Lost in Meditation

The fresh arrows spreading endlessly
The feast of green sparkling with delight.

Large trees are dreaming a historical dream
With a bright sky overhead.

Their roots spread deeply,
The breath of their sap
Rising from their veins.

Putting their heart in a point
For one hundred years,
They add an annual ring.

나무의 운명

어둠 속에서 총 쏘듯 튀어나와
푸른 바다에 빠져버렸다
혼자 서서만 있어야 하는 운명

친구들과 서로서로
등 긁어주며 자라기로 하였다
햇빛과 바람이 겨드랑이 간질이는
시간에 키가 자라고
새가 날아가는 시간에 꽃이 피었다

오직 하늘 향해 손을 들고
반대도 찬성도 없이 옳소만 하고 있다

때로는 비바람에 도리질을 할 때에도
자리 옮기려 하지 않고 자리를 지킨다

적막한 날들에 흘러가는 시간들을
심장 속에 새기며 내 자리를 지킨다

Tree's Fate

A tiny sprout shoots up
To become a member of the green world
With the fate of standing alone.

She makes some friends
Who scratch her where she itches;
She grows
While sunlight and wind tickle her under the arm;
She makes flowers
While birds are singing.

She just looks up to the sky putting her hands up;
She doesn't know how to object,
Just saying, "Yes."

She keeps her seat
While getting caught in a rainstorm.

Even in a long silence,
She engraves passing days on her heart.

아름다운 사람

오늘 아침 웃는 얼굴 아름다워라
먼저 비켜 서 주는 마음 아름다워라
겸손히 배려하는 자세 아름다워라

평행선을 달리는 기나긴 여로
만날 듯 스칠 때 사랑을 하고
허허로운 마음 서로 위로하며

오늘도 긴 기적소리 빈자리를 채우고
일상에 지친 영혼들 살며시 위로하며
무거운 삶의 무게를 지하철에 싣는다

2021년 서울지하철 공모 시 당선작

The Lovely Person

The face that smiles in the morning is so beautiful,
The heart that steps aside is so beautiful,
The attitude that is considerate for others is so beautiful.

A long journey running in parallel
Is a relationship just passing by, but with affection,
Comforting each other's empty feelings.

The long train whistle fills today's empty space,
It gently consoles the souls who are tired of the daily life,
Carrying the weight of life on the subway.

t is a prize-winning entry in the 2021 contest held by Seoul Metropolitan Subway.

꽃들에게

아침이 열리면 파릇한 새싹으로
우리에게 기쁜 마음 움트게 하고

이슬 머금으며 힘차게 뻗는 잎들
희망으로 우리를 꿈꾸게 하더니

세상을 품은 듯 앙증맞은 봉오리
사람들 가슴을 벅차게 하는구나

제비 입 닮아 하나 둘 벌어지는
꽃잎들은 향기로운 천사의 날개

너희들이 펼치는 꽃 잔치는
별들이 펼치는 우주의 신비로움

아련한 향수 속에 피는 수선화
옛 님 못 잊어 애   은 물망초

파르르 떨며 화려한 얼굴 요염한 양귀비
겸손한 잎들 무수히 함께 피어나는 백일홍

봄에는 갸날프나 성숙해지는 바늘꽃의 화려함
하늘하늘 가을하늘 수놓는 코스모스

찬서리 이기고 피어나는 국화꽃의 겸손함
이 계절이 지나가면 너 또한 떠나가겠지만

또 다시 돌아오는 봄
또 다시 화려한 향기로

또 다시 아름다운 얼굴로
꼭 다시 돌아와 꽃 잔치 열어주렴

To Flowers

When the morning opens,
Your green shoots bloom in our happy hearts;

Your dewy leaves that stretch out vigorously
Make us dream with hope;

Your cute buds that seem to embrace the world
Make our hearts flutter:

Your petals spreading their lips one by one like swallows' mouths
Are the wings of a fragrant angel;

The flower party you throw is
The mystery of the universe by the stars;

The daffodil that makes you nostalgic;
The sad forget-me-not that can't forget its old love;

The fluttering and flamboyant poppy shaking their fancy faces;
The zinnia elegance with humble petals blooming together;

The willow herb that is slender in spring, but becomes colorful;
The cosmos that sways embroidering autumn sky;

The humble chrysanthemum that blooms overcoming cold frost;
When this season passes, you will also leave,

Spring will come back
With a flashy scent again.

Please come back with your beautiful faces
And have a flower party for us again.

인생 *Life*

사랑은 흐른다 ④

여의도 단상

사방에 산이 있어 오르지 못할 이 없고
사방에 산이 있어 보지 못할 이 없다

그 산은 호랑이도 감추고 살쾡이도 기른다
그 산은 반달곰도 기르고 스컹크도 감춘다

삼면에 바다가 있어 누구라도 바다에 간다
삼면에 바다가 있어 누구라도 배를 띄운다

가다가 풍랑이 일면 권력으로 잠재우고
가다가 폭풍 오면 공양미 삼천삼백 석

인당수 푸른 물에

호랑이도 빠지고 살쾡이도 뛰어들고
반달곰도 뛰어들고 스컹크도 빠지고
뛰어들고 빠지고 지독한 냄새

푸른 기와집 맹인잔치에
심청이 연꽃 태워 환생시킬 용왕님도
지레 질식사하면 이를 어찌하리

Stray Thoughts on Yeouido

There are mountains all over
So there is nobody who cannot climb them,
Or nobody who cannot see them.

The mountains provide shelter to tigers and skunks;
They also raise wildcats and bears.

We are surrounded by water on three sides
So everyone can set a boat afloat.

When a storm comes up,
They can calm it down by using power,
Or by offering a bribe
Like 3,300 bags of rice offered to Buddha.

The blue river is named Indangsu;

Many animals fall into the water,
Such as tigers, wildcats, bears, and skunks,
Giving out a bad smell.
If the Dragon King of the sea would be suffocated
By the smell,

Who can resuscitate Simcheong who are riding on a lotus
To let her give a feast for the blind
In a big and blue tile-roofed house?

迷路

깨어 있지도 잠들지도 못하는
세상은 모두가 가로등인가
곧게 뻗어 있어도
곧게 갈 수 없는 길
세상은 모두가 꼬부랑길인가

길 없는 길 걸어온 나그네에게
신새벽 눈 비비는 햇살은 바늘을 품고
삐뚜루 와버린 벼랑길 되돌릴 수 없어
허둥대는 마음을 찌르고 다시 찌르고

차라리 길 없는 광야에다
길을 만들고
곧게 걸으려고 걸으려고

그래도 가다가다
휘고 또 휘어지면
흔적 없이 사라지라
길이 나에게 말하네

Miro

The world is a streetlight
Because it doesn't go to bed
Or wake up;
The world is a winding path
Because people walk in a zigzag
Along its straight way.

In the morning
The sunlight beats down
Seemingly stabbing the wanderers,
Who have walked flounderingly
Along the pathless berm.

People think that they'd rather make a way
In the wild pathless field
Than walk along the right path.

However, their way bends
Again and again.
Sometimes, the path seems to say to me,
Disappear without a trace.

悔恨

오르지도 못할 나무 쳐다보다 굴러 떨어진
높이 오른 龍 그리려다 지렁이도 못 그린
푼수 같은

앞山에 뜨는 해 마주 보아 눈이 시어서
진정 보아야 할 것 보지 못하고
뜨거우면 녹아내리는
이카루스의 날개 같은
세상살이를

건성으로 애 돌아온 육십삼 년
올 수도 갈 수도 없는 지점에
이르러 어찌하랴
웃어야 울어야 참아야 할지

하얀 새벽 검은 밤을 하나로 묶어
햇살처럼 머리 빗기는 우물 속에
넣고 헹구어
갈 길 밝힐 수만 있다면
차라리 내 가지 않은 길에 등불을
꼼꼼히 비추련만

A Keen Regret

I was an idiot
Who wanted to draw a dragon
That rose to the sky,
But drew only an earthworm.

Our life is an Icarus' wing
That melted down
Because of flying too high,
Close to the sun,
So I became too blind to see
What I had to see.

63 years have passed absentmindedly;
And I am standing at the point
Where I don't know
If I should go forward or return back,
Or if I should laugh or cry.

If I can put the times together,
I want to put them into the well
And wash them clean
To make the road ahead bright.

바람

크나큰 산 흔들 수 없어
안달하는 너

골짜기 휘돌아
크나큰 나무 옮기려 해도
밑동은 꿈쩍도 않아

바람아 너는 어디서 살아?
푸르고 높은 하늘 위?
아니면 어둡고 깊은 바닷속?

바람이 나에게 묻네

그럼 너는 어디서 살아?

나는 몰라 여기가 어딘지
검은 구름 속인지
깊고 깊은 산골짜기인지

차라리 아무것도 없음에
너의 있음을 느낀다

The Wind

You are trying hard
To shake huge mountains,
Or to move big trees,
But they are motionless.

Hey, are you living
In the high blue sky,
Or in the depths of the dark sea?

You ask me back,

Where are you living, then?

I don't know where I am.
Am I in the dark cloud,
Or in an abysmal ravine?

I have come to know your existence
Here Where there is nothing.

인생

인생
그것은 바람이라네

인생
그것은
영롱한 빛으로
한번 떴다 사라지는 무지개라네

인생
그것은
한때 향기로 머물다
바람에 흩어지는 꽃잎이라네

그래도 그것을 위하여
오늘도 구르고 내일도 뛰는 것

또한 그것이 인생이라네

Life

Life is like the wind.

It is like a rainbow
Which appears brilliantly
And then disappears pretty soon.

It is like a flower
Sending forth fragrance once
And then scattering in the wind.

They roll today
And run for it tomorrow.

That is life.

안개 같은 인생

가로등 불빛을
너의 몸뚱이로 휘감고
성난 파도인양
밤공기를 뒤흔드는

나의 두 눈마저
가려버리는

한밤을 소리 없이 휘젓는
뿌리 없는 너는 누구인가

한없이 흩어져버린 삶
조각들이 제 짝을 못 찾아
울고 헤맬 때

한 번도 그들에게
말할 수 없었던

한평생 흔적 없이
배회해야 하는 고향 없는
너는 누구인가

노오란 가로등 불빛에
마녀처럼 산발한 너의 머리를
못 빗기우듯

엉킨 실타래 된 내 삶 꼬리를 찾아
오늘도 내일도 헤매고

연기처럼 해체된 내 영혼
오늘 밤은 어디로
가야 할지 망설이고

너를 따라 흐르듯

우리 아름다운 세월
낙엽 뒤로 숨어버리고

하얀 안개꽃처럼 아스러지면
그때 어찌 피어나길 기도한다네

Life Is Like A Fog

Who are you
That has no roots
But wraps the street lights,
Shakes the night air
Like angry waves,
And even covers up my eyes?

Who are you
With never a home,
But that wanders with tears,
Holding slices of life?

I have no person to whom
I can express my feelings.

I look for my tangled skein of life,
Like the disheveled hair of a witch,
Over the yellow light,
Today and maybe tomorrow also.

Not knowing where to go,
I stray along beside you
In the night
With my disintegrated soul.

Although that wonderful time has crumbled
And has gone with the fallen leaves,
I pray it will bloom again
Like a white baby's breath.

세상 살기

마음속 분노가
거세게 일 때
더 큰 인내가
필요하고

마음의 평정을
잃을 때
더 큰 냉정함이
필요하다네

세상 우물이
깊고 깊을 때
탈출은 더더욱
쉽지 않다네

푸른 잎새
속에서
파란 벌레
찾기 쉽지 않고

진분홍 꽃잎 속에서
피멍을 찾기 힘드네
우리의 삶도
무엇이 그리 쉬울까

The Way of Living

When you feel in your heart
The swelling of indignation,
A lot of patience is needed.

When you lose
Peace of mind,
You try to regain your composure
At once.

When you sink deep
In the mire of the world,
It is so hard
To get out of it.

It is not easy
To find a green bug
In the green foliage;

It is hard to tell a bruise
From red petals,
Life is much more like this.

절망과 희망

차가운 바람은
우리에게 속삭이며 스쳐간다
깊은 절망에서
희망을 노래하라고

그리곤 하이얀 눈을
흩뿌려댄다
희망이 여기 아직
살아 있노라고

잿빛 하늘은
나직이 떠돌며 속삭인다
나 여기 이렇게
아직 살아 있노라고

구두 뒷굽에
질척거리며 매달려 가는
희망의 조각들이
차츰 그 힘을 잃어갈 때

절망은 말한다
절망은 절대로 절망이 아니라고

우리는 이렇게
절망과 희망을 바라보며
긴-긴 날을 바람처럼 살아왔다

1990년도
2000년도
2010년도
3020년도
우리는 또 그렇게 살아갈 것이다

Despair and Hope

The chilly wind passes over,
Saying, “Sing hope
Even in times of deep despair.”

And the wind scatters flurries of snow,
Saying, “Hope stays alive here.”

The gray cloud lying low whispers,
Saying, “Here hope is still alive.”

By the time the pieces of hope
Are beginning to lose their strength,
Hanging on by the heel of their shoes,

Despair says
Despair is never despair.

We have lived like the wind
For a long long time,
Longing for despair and hope,

We lived like this
In 1990,
In 2000,
And in 2010.

We will also live like this
In 3020.

회색 봄

안개바람인가 황사바람인가
아리 아리 어리 어리

세상도 안개에 마음도 황사에
또렷한 일 하나도 없네

그래도 깃발 흔들리고 바람개비 돌고 있네
누구를 위하여인지도 모르고

어설픈 안개로 세상이 덮여가고
봄이면 오는 황사는 바람인가

핏빛으로 다가오던 진홍색 봄꽃이
어지러운 아지랑이 품에서 기절을 하고

나른하게 다가오는 봄 뻐꾸기 소리
아른거리는 세상과 어디서 만나야 하나

Grey Spring

Is it a misty wind or
A yellow dust wind?
Ari ari, all dim!

Like the world shrouded in mist,
Like people's hearts covered with yellow dust,
There is not anything that is definite.

The pinwheel spins alone
Without knowing for whom it spins.

The world becomes covered
With an ambiguous mist,
Every spring suffering from the yellow dust wind.

The crimson flowers, just coming out,
Feel dizzy because of the simmering heat.

The cuckoo's song, singing for spring,
Just sounds drowsy in the flickering world.

한여름 장마

천둥 번개 짝 되어
나들이 오면
빗줄기가 그려놓은
한여름의 수채화
그것은 아슴푸레한 잿빛이었네

억수같이 쏟아 붓는 폭포수
집도 차도 떠내려 보낼
바다 만들고
황톳물에 엉켜버린
우리들의 삶

싯누런 강바닥에서
건져 보는 희망
언제나 참고 기다리라는
격언만이
낮은 곳에 둥지 튼
서민들 몫이라네

Rainy Spells in Summer

With lighting and thunder's coming
For a date,
Rain streaks greyly like paint with watercolors
In high summer.

The heavy rain causes floods
That wash away houses and cars.
Lives of people struggle
In red clay water.

Their trying to fish hope
Out of the vivid yellow water
Comes to naught.
The proverb, "Sweet after bitter!"
Always falls to the poor's share,
Who built their nest in the lower spot.

송파

아스라이 안개에 덮여
꿈을 꾸고 있는 마을

흙으로 쌓은 몽촌토성
두고 온 고향 생각케 하는 곳

태고의 시원으로부터
흘러온 옛 강이 오늘도 흐르듯

선조들의 유구한
역사와 문화유산
면면히 살아 숨 쉬는 곳

그곳에서 해바라기
장미꽃 피우고
함박웃음 지으며
사랑을 배우고
더 큰 사랑 하라며
채찍질도 받았네

오늘도 석촌 호수
붉은 꽃에 물들고
맑은 휘파람 소리
하늘 높이 퍼지네

Songpa

The fog-shrouded dreaming village,
Surrounded by earthen ramparts.

It reminds me of my home
Where I left my heart.

The place where our ancestors still live on
Through their rich history
And cultural heritage
Like a river running
From time immemorial.

I would accept chastening from here
To learn how to love more fully
With a great big smile,
That brings roses and sunflowers.

Seokchon Lake is as beautiful as ever
Tinged with the red of the flowers;
A clear ringing whistle is resounding.

남편

희끗 희끗한 머리를 뒤로 빗어 올리며
거울을 보는 당신의 뒷모습

젊은 날의 푸른 기운이 조금은 느껴질까
가만히 들여다 본다

세 살 적 어머니 품을
떠나 외로움 견디며
용케도 이 험한 세상을 헤쳐 온 당신

누구에게 질세라 누가 될세라
더 열심히 일하고 더 열심히 살아온 당신

옆에 어려운 사람 보이면 먼저 손잡아 주고

조금도 고마움 모르는 혈육을 천륜이라 여기며
끝없이 끝없이 베푸는 그 따뜻한 마음

당신이 있어 이 세상을 떳떳하게 살았고

당신이 있어 이 세상을 의미 있게 살았고

당신과 함께 이 세상을 행복하게 살았어요

Husband

The back of you looking in the mirror
While combing your grizzled hair back,

You look carefully into it, wondering
If you can feel the green light of your youth.

Apart from your mother’s arms when you were three,
You've endured the loneliness and
Managed to get through this tough world.

You have been living and working harder
Afraid of losing to or putting pressure on others.

If you see someone having a hard time, you hold his hand before anyone else.

Even if your family members don't thank you at all,
Saying that you can’t give up morals, you just give them endlessly with a warm heart.

Thanks to you, I've lived in this world proudly,

Because of you, I've lived a meaningful life,

I've lived happily ever after because I was with you.

어긋난 세상

저 푸른 바닷물은 짜고도 짠데
그 바다에 사는 물고기는 짜지가 않네

저 파란 하늘은 파랗고도 파란데
저 파란 하늘을 나는 새들은 파랗지가 않네

저 산의 나무는 푸르고도 푸른데
그 푸른 나무에서 피는 꽃은 푸르지가 않네

우리가 살아가는 날들은 길고도 긴데
그 삶 속에 날들은 짧기만 하네

진정한 사랑이란 달콤하고도 아름다운데
그 진정한 사랑은 아프고도 슬프네

Misaligned World

The blue sea water is salty and salty,
But the fish living there are not salty.

The sky is blue and blue,
But the birds flying there are not blue.

The trees in the mountain are green and green,
But the flowers blooming there are not green.

The days we will live are long and long,
But the days of our lives are short.

True love is sweet and beautiful,
But the true love hurts and is sad.

스쳐 지나가는 것들

푸르른 날들이 지나 간다
빽빽하던 잎이 하나 둘 자리를 비운다

푸르른 날들이 지나간다
파랗던 잎들이 노랗게 물들어 간다

푸르르던 날들이 지나갔다
청춘의 빛나는 얼굴로 인생이 기쁘던 시절

푸르르던 시절이 지나갔다
황홀한 사랑으로 온 세상이 분홍빛으로 물들었던

푸르르던 시절이 지나갔다
새 생명을 품에 안고 심장 뛰던 그 시간들

푸르르던 시절이 지나갔다
나를 닮은 아이들 무럭무럭 자라 가슴 뿌듯한 시절

푸르르던 시절이 지나간다
빛과 그림자 환희 사랑 그리고 외로움

그 푸르르던 시절의 지나감으로
은빛 노을과 황금빛 노을 사이에

지워지지 않는 무늬와 빛깔로
채색된 한 폭의 그림이 떠 있다

Things That Pass by

Green days pass by,
Dense leaves leave one by one.

Green days pass by,
The green leaves are turning yellow.

Green days passed by,
When life was happy with a young radiant face.

Green days passed by,
When the whole world was dyed pink with ecstatic love.

Green days passed by,
When my heart beat with a new life in my arms.

Green days passed by,
When I was proud of my mini-me children growing up.

Green days passed by,

When light and shadow, joy and loneliness were together.

Due to the green days that passed by,

Between the silver sunset and the golden sunset,

There is a picture of

An indelible pattern and color.

펄럭이는 태극기 앞에

무궁화 줄지어 핀 언덕에
태극기가 펄럭 입니다

펄럭이는 태극기 앞에
가슴에 손을 얹고 하늘을 우러러 봅니다

이 태극기 하나를 지키기 위해
얼마나 많은 피를 흘리고 목숨을 바쳤던가

애국심을 기르려면 현충원을 와 보아라
태극기 대한민국 우리나라 나의조국

그러나 아직도 끝나지 않은 전쟁
나쁜 평화는 죽음보다 못하다고 외치는
우리들의 애국심은 흐느낀다

아직도 산화한 전사자의 유해를
말없이 맞이하는 동작동 국립현충원
장엄한 미사의 서곡 뒤 애국가가 연주된다

조국을 지키기 위해 한줌의 흙이 되었을 지라도
그는 이곳에서 또 조국을 지키는 별이 되리라

가슴에 손을 얹고 무궁화 줄지어 핀 언덕에 서서
푸른 하늘에 펄럭이는 태극기를 우러러 본다

In Front of the Fluttering Korean Flag,

The flag flutters
On the hill lined with Mugunghwa.

In front of the fluttering flag,
I put my hand on my chest and look up to the sky.

To protect this Korean flag,
How many people were bleeding and sacrificing their lives?

If you want to develop patriotism, come to the Memorial Hall, Where there's the Korean flag, your country, Republic of Korea.

Then, the war still hasn't ended.
Our patriotism cries out that
Bad peace is worse than death.

The national anthem performance continues after the solemn prelude at Dongjak-dong National Cemetery, which still welcomes with reverence the remains of the dead.

Even if they became a handful of soil after protecting their country,
They will be the stars that protect their country here again.

Standing on a hill lined with Mugunghwa with hands on my chest,
I look up to our national flag fluttering in the blue sky.

사랑 Love

사랑은 흐른다 ⑤

사랑

사랑은

꽃이다
별이다
꿈이다

사랑은

바람이다
소나기다
무지개다

그리고
잊혀지지 않는 동굴이다

Love

Love is

A flower,
A star,
A dream.

Love is

A wind,
A shower,
A rainbow.

And
A hunting cave.

나의 어머니

어머니
신새벽 찬 서리 밟고
흰 광목 치마
깃발처럼 펄럭이며
좁은 골목 물동이 이고
걸어오던 당신

어머니
토담 곁에 내려앉은
열 길 깊은 우물물 길어
모든 것 다 주어도
한없이 모자라
목숨까지라도 주고 싶은
당신의 마음

어머니
보리개떡 쑥버무리
나물죽에 고구마도
사랑 많은 당신 있어 든든했지요
떨어진 검정 고무신을
안타까이 기워주던 그 손길 있어
맨발에 자갈밭도
씩씩하게 걸어왔지요

어머니
빗겨간 푸른 날들이 이마에 나이테를 그리고
아름답던 젊은 날이 돋보기에 아른거릴 때
검푸르던 당신의 머리에 어느새 내려앉은
하이얀 세월의 흔적

어머니
이제 당신의 들판은
풍성한 수확을 끝내고
더 아름다운 열매를 맺기 위해
다음해를 기다립니다

My mother

Mother,
I remember the frosty early mornings
When you walked the alley
Setting a water jar on your head
In your white cotton skirt ruffling
In the cold wind like a flag.

Mother,
Now I understand your mind
That was not content with drawing water
From ten fathoms deep.
You wanted to give even your life
For your family.

Mother,
Though I made do with coarse cakes
Made of barley or mugwort,
Vegetable porridge, or sweet potatoes,
I felt full when you were with me;
Though I walked down the gravelly field,
With torn rubber shoes on,
Your warm healing hand gave me courage.

Mother,
On your forehead,
There are more lines for each year,
Made up of your bygone, younger days.
On your white hair,
There are traces of time descended.

My mother,
After having a successful harvest,
Your field is waiting
For another season
To bear more beautiful fruit.

결혼축시 - 사랑

내 가슴에 찬란한 별
오직 그대 나의 별

하늘 보며 그리움으로 밤을 지새워도
분홍빛 가슴이 환희로 가득 차고

초록빛 꿈을 꾸며 새집을 지을 때
그대는 그 집의 영원한 주인이라

흐르는 세월 속에 비바람 몰아치고
크고 험한 산, 깊고 푸른 강을 건너야 할 때도 있으리라

그래도 그 집은 이 세상 어느 곳보다 따뜻하고
꿈결과 같은 사랑이 함께하는 곳이라

그대 둘 이제는 하나 되어
새로운 세상 열어 펼쳐 갈 테니

그 길은 꽃처럼 바람처럼
감미롭고 향기로워라

아 사랑이여 신부 신랑여!
식을 줄 모르는 꿈같은 이 둘의 사랑

영원히 영원히
이 세상 끝까지 지켜 주소서

Epithalamium - Love

A glittering star is in my heart;
It is you of all the stars.

A glittering star is in my heart;
It is you of all the stars.

You will be the only owner
Of our new home, ever,
Made with our green dreams.

Though there will be days
We have to go over rough and high mountains
And to across deep and surfy water,
We will feel the warmth and love in our home
That we've never felt in another place.

Two of us become one from now
And open a new world.

The way of the world
Will give us a mellowness and sweetness.

Oh, we are a lovely bride and groom;
May this dreamlike love keep warm forever!

May we cherish this love
Even unto the end of the world!

못다 한 사랑

가슴에서
불어오는 회오리바람에 눈을 감는다
대평원을 가로지르는 크고 깊은 야크의 발자국
검은 우주 한 켠에 시공을 넘나드는 티끌로
영원히 풀리지 않는 수수께끼를 찾아 스무고개를 한다

아직도
살아온 날과 살아갈 날이 같다고
다시 살아갈 날들을 준비한다
아침 햇살 스며드는 핑크빛 커튼 사이로
회생을 꿈꾸며 밤이면 포개져 사랑을 하고
낮이면 애달파 하는 자귀꽃으로

그러나
황무지 텅 빈 언덕으로 서리서리 몰려오던
모랫바람 위에 켜켜이 앉아버린 세월의 눈물
퇴색한 물감처럼 희미한 그림자 속에
미처 다 알지 못한 사랑의 의미

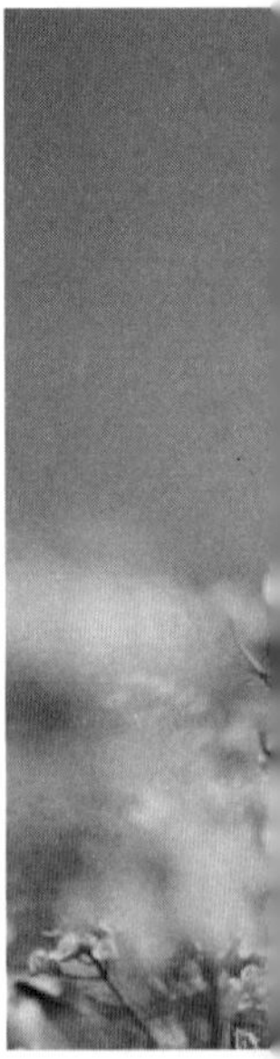

이제는
가버린 이 하얀 억새꽃으로 길 위에 머물고
더 이상 뜨겁게 다가오지 않을 맞바람으로 하여
그동안 가슴에 담아두었던 이들을 하나 둘 버리고 간다

Unfinished Love

It is a tornado rising in my heart;
It is a big and deep footprint of a yak
In the great plain;
It is a speck transcending time and space
In a corner of the vast black universe;
It is the deepest mystery forever.

It is like the silk tree leaves,
Over the pink curtain in the morning sun,
Who laid one upon another last night
Dreaming of the recovery of love,
Yet their hearts will break during the daytime.
In the half way point between the days left to live
And the days I've lived;
I get myself together to prepare for the days to live.

It is like the dried tears
Piled up on the barren hill
A long time that were caused by the sandstorm;
It is a discolored picture, a vague shape
Faded before knowing the meaning of love.

It is like a back wind
That will never come again burningly,
But will stay in the road of the silver grass.
I am going to leave, leaving the beloved ones there.

가을 사랑

내가 험난한 이 세상
맨 처음 걸음마 할 때
손잡아 이끌어 준 이
높은 하늘 같았고

내가 험난한 이 세상
맨 처음 헤엄칠 때
달콤한 키스로
행복하게 한 이 바다 같아라

이제 험하디험한
이 어두운 바다에서
풍랑 만나 좌초되고
광풍 만나 뒤집혀도

따뜻이 손잡고
달콤한 키스 나눌 이 없으니
나의 하늘 바다 되어줄 이
아무도 없으니

사랑도 봄이요
가을은 아니어라
하물며 차디찬 겨울에
사랑이 있으랴

Love of Fall

The love that held my hand,
When I took a first step
In this tough world,
That love was sky-high.

The love that gave me a warm kiss,
When I strove
Through the world's waves;
That love was as deep as the sea.

Now I am stranded
And turned over
By a violent storm
In the rough and dark sea.

However,
There is no one
Who gives me a kiss of comfort,
Grabbing onto my hand tightly.

Now
The spring of love has gone,
Leaving behind only the love of fall.
Moreover, is there any love in the cold winter?

생의 향기

봄이 되면
내 집 앞 길가에
벤치를 놓고
오고 가는 사람
쉬게 할 테요

봄이 되면
내 집 앞 가로수 밑에
화분을 놓고
오고 가는 사람
보게 할 테요

봄이 되면
내 집 앞 처마 끝에
바람개비를 달고
오고 가는 사람
휘파람 불게 할 테요

봄이 되면
내 집 앞뜰에 유채를 심고
오고 가는 벌 나비
설레게 할 테요

바람처럼 흩어지는
생의 향취를

벤치 되고
화분 되고
바람개비 벌 나비 되어
휘파람으로 흩어지지 않게
꼭꼭 붙잡아 볼 테요

Scents of Life

When spring comes,
I am going to set out a bench
In front of my house
For passersby to rest on.

When spring comes,
I am going to place potted flowers
Under the street trees
For passersby to enjoy.

When spring comes,
I am going to put pinwheels
On the eaves
For passersby to blow whistles
To the tune of them.

When spring comes,
I am going to plant canola
For the hearts of bees and butterflies
To leap up.

I want to grasp the scents of life
So they won't to scatter like the wind.

I want to become a bench,
A potted flower,
A pinwheel,
A bee, or a butterfly
That never vanishes on a whistle.

우정

우리의 영과 육이
성장을 필요로 할 때
우리는 한몸처럼
환희와 슬픔을
함께했었다
낮과 밤을 같이 뒹굴며

아스라이 멀어져간
시간 속에서
간신히 건져 올린
우정이란 사진첩
삼십 년의 세월 속에
무엇이 남아있던가

너의 잘린 손마디에
우리의 가슴앓이가
나의 아름다운
찬송가 선율에
그 시절 함께 외치던
고학의 합창소리가 묻어 있음을
우리가 아니고
그 누가 알고 있으랴

친구여!
나의 사랑하는 친구여!
머나먼 삶의 길에
때론 외롭고 서럽더라도
우리 함께 있음을

사랑하는 여인이
나만을 위하여 존재한다고
착각하듯이 그렇게 그렇게
아픔의 추억으로
사랑의 추억으로 살아가자
벗이여!

Friendship

When we needed to be nurtured
Spiritually and physically,
We came together,
As if we were one,
Day and night,
Sharing joy and sorrow.

So long,
Thirty years later,
What can I still find
In the photo album
Named Friendship?

Your rough knuckle is a testament
To the trials we went through;
Seeing me singing hymns speaks
Of our hopeful songs
We would shout together,
Trying to survive the daily grind,
As working students
Who having hard times that cannot be shared in common.

Friend,
My dear friend,
Don’t lose courage,
Though your life’s journey is weary,
’Cause we are together always!

Live like the lovers who believe that
The other party exists for themselves;
Lead our life
Keeping our minds upon
The happy and sad memories,
My buddy!

행복

산그늘 깊은 못에
천 년을 잠겨
기나긴 꿈을 꾸는
이무기같이

사랑의 긴 여울이
흐르는 강에
나직이 내려앉은
물안개같이

기쁨이 파도 치는
가없는 바다 위에
하이얀 깃발 달은
돛단배같이

새소리 고즈넉한
들녘에 서서
전원 교향곡 선율로
피어난 들꽃과 같이

우리에게 행복이란 영원한 샘물

Happiness

It is like Imoogi*
Who dreams a long dream
Sinking in a deep mountain pond
For thousands of years.

It is like wet fog
Which wraps gently
Over the long running river
Of love.

It is like a sailing ship
With a white banner waving,
Floating on the endless sea
Where the waves of joy dance.

It is like a wild flower
Blooming in a peaceful field
Enjoying the song of birds
As Pastoral.

It is like spring water
That never ever dries.

* A legendary animal

타지마할

천국의 정원 아그라 야무나강에
그림자도 아름다운 사랑의 증표

한 남자의 뜨거운 사랑
하얗게 빛나는 마음
오늘도 푸른 연못
붉은 꽃 속에
그들은 살아있었네

그 누가 사랑은
한순간 가슴속에 부는
바람이라 하였는가

400년을 한결같이
푸르도록
하이얀 대리석으로

사랑이 영원함을 증명하는
샤자한과 뭄타즈마할

후세에 이 자리에 선 우리들
어디에서 이런 사랑 찾아야 하나

Taj Mahal

A garden of heaven,
By the Yamuna River in Agra,
A token of love;
Even its silhouette is beautiful.

The burning love and beaming heart
Of a man
Still live in the red flowers
And the green pond.

Who said
Love is a wind
Rising in the heart
For some time?

The white marble glowing
For 400 years
Shows that love is everlasting.

Shah Jahan and Mumtaz Mahal
Proves eternal love.

Where can we find this love
In this day and age?

꿈

물 첩첩 산 첩첩
오므린 손바닥 안에서
시공을 초월하는
자유를 꿈꾸며
차오르는 열정으로
비상하는 한 마리 종달새

젊은 날
꽃도 별도 한 아름
터질 듯 가슴에 안고
두려움 모르고
세상에 맞섰다

비바람 세차게
몰아치는 광야에서도
쉬지 않고 달리는 뜨거움
그 깊은 뿌리는 고향이었네
초심 살아 있는 첩첩산중
내 고향

Dream

I was a sky lark
Who tried to fly up into the sky
Dreaming of freedom passionately,
Transcending time and space
From the innermost tiny village of a mountain.

In my youth
I encountered the world
Without any fear,
With an armful
Of flowers and stars.

Although it was in a secluded valley,
Thanks to my hometown,
A sure anchor of my soul
Kept my first resolution,
So I could run through the roaring wilderness.

부부의 연

푸르렀던 젊은날
흰가운을 입은 제약회사 같은 직장에서
두메산골 촌색시와 서울 토박이 남자가 만났다

서울 토박이 남자는 때 묻지 않은 시골 처녀의
웃는 모습이 예쁘다며 청혼을 했다

두메산골 처녀는 도시 처녀들처럼 계산도 할 줄 모르고
자기를 좋다고 하는 그 남자의 청혼을 받아들였다

두 사람은 단칸 셋방도 궁궐처럼 생각하고
줄줄이 딸린 식솔들을 건사하며 두 아이를 낳아 길렀다

두 사람은 아주 작은 곳에서 더 큰 세상을 향해 꿈을 키우고
있는 그 순간에 열정적으로 최선을 다 하였다

삶이라는 바다에서 서로의 마음이 다를 때도 있었고
이 놀이를 그만두고 싶을 때도 있었다

서 있는 곳이 너무 척박하여 때로는 힘들고 서럽기도 했다
그러나 참고 또 참고 지내다 보니 어느새 하늘이 보였다

이제 단풍든 언덕에 올라 지난날을 돌아보니
그를 만난 것은 이번 생에 있어 크나큰 행운이었고

결코 결코 계산을 잘 못한 것이 아니었다

Matrimonial Ties

On a young day
While working in a white gown at a pharmaceutical company,
A girl from a rural mountain village and a native Seoul guy met.

The man proposed to her, saying that
The unspoiled country girl's smile was pretty.

The girl accepted the proposal of the man who said he liked her,
Not knowing how to calculate as much as the city girls.

The couple thought of a single room as a palace and
Raised two children while supporting many other in-law.

The couple developed their dreams from that tiny place toward a bigger world,
Doing their best passionately at the moment they faced it.

In the sea of life, there were times when the couple had different idea,
and There were times when they wanted to quit the game.

The place where they were standing was so barren that
sometimes they felt exhausted and sad.
However, as they endured and endured, they could see the sky.

Climbing up the hill colored with autumn leaves,
Looking back on the past, the girl feels that meeting the man
was a great luck in her life,

That she had never done anything wrong with the calculation.

장마

우렁 우렁 하늘 울고
주렁 주렁 내리는 비
주먹 처럼 큰 주먹비
내가 가꾸어 놓은 봉숭아 채송화
가냘픈 꽃들 다 때려 눕혀 버리네

이른 봄 씨를 뿌릴 때부터
기다려 온 꽃들이 방긋

방긋이 화알짝 웃으려는데
난데없는 물 폭탄에

쓰러지는 이들을 보며
안쓰러워 애타는 마음

화분에 심은 꽃들은
사람 쉬는 곳으로 피난시키고

제자리 앉은 것들은 속절없이
비속에서 아우성이다

어찌하랴 하늘에서 하는 일을
사람의 힘으로 어찌 하리오

Monsoon Rain

The sky is crying loud and loud,
It's raining hard and hard,
Raindrops that are as big as fists are tearing away
All my slender flowers, such as balsam and rose mosses blossoms.

The seeds that have been waiting since they were sowed in early spring Bloom
into flowers and smile.

When they are about to smile broadly,
The water bombs fall out of nowhere.

Looking at the falling flowers,
My heart just aches.

The flowers planted in the pot
Managed to escape to a place where people rest.

The others sitting in their place
Are clamoring in the rain.

What can we do about what heaven does?
How can we handle it with human power?

백로

여러분!!
여기에 하얀 백로가 와요!!

커다란 순백의 날개를
차양처럼 펼치고

좁은 하늘가를 맴돌다
살며시 내려 앉아

시냇물에 긴 발 담그고
수면 속 얼굴과 입 맞춤 하네요

여러분!!

여기에 꿈속의 천사처럼
하이얀 백로가 와요!!

White Heron

Hey,
A white heron is coming here!

Spreading its pure white wings
Like a sunshade,

Hovering in the narrow air and
Gently sitting down,

Finally, it puts its long feet in the stream and
Kisses its beak reflected in the water.

Hey,

An angel-like white heron
Comes here!

창밖의 오동나무

큰 새 먼저 오면 작은 새 갸웃 갸웃
하늘 향한 아름드리 기운 찬 자태
무성한 잎 떨 구니 산새들 놀이터

푸르고 검은 구름 온 몸으로 감싸며
비 바람 소리 속으로 속으로 담아

가야금 비파 소리
시집 간 여인네 애닮은 마음

애절하고 아름다운 음률
세상에 내어놓는 그를 닮으라

The Paulownia Tree Outside the Window

A big bird sits down on you first, and even a small bird snoops.
You, making a beautiful figure towards the sky,
Dropping a lot of leaves, become a playground for birds.

You cover the dark blue clouds with your whole body,
Contain the sounds of rain and wind in you,

Produce the sounds of gayageum and lute to capture
The heart of a woman leading a hard married life.

We should emulate you who gives the world
A sad and beautiful melody.

양귀비 꽃

형형색색 천하일색
교교히 아름다운 자태

작은 바람에도 나비 유혹하며
얇은 꽃잎은 파르르 떨고

겹쳐 입은 듯 한 속잎
주름 잡혀 입체감을 더하고

섬세한 꽃술은 속살을 보여주듯
수줍게 교태를 부리고

과연 진시황의 양귀비처럼
보는 이들 마음 설레게 한다

Poppy

A mass of color, the fairest of fairest,
The sophisticated and beautiful figure!

Even in the small wind, her thin petals
Become a butterfly that trembles and seduces.

Her inner leaves, which look like they're overlapped,
Are wrinkled, adding a three-dimensional effect.

Her delicate pistil is shy
As if she shows flesh.

Like Qin Shi Huang's Poppy,
She makes viewers' hearts flutter.

자취

꽃이 핀 자리
꽃이 진 자리
꽃이 떨어진 자리

사람이 난 자리
사람이 된 자리
사람이 진 자리

그곳에는
무엇이 남을까

Trace

The place where a flower bloomed;
The place where a flower withered;
The place where a flower fell.

The place where a person has come;
The place where a person has had personality;
The place where a person has gone.

What trace will be left there?

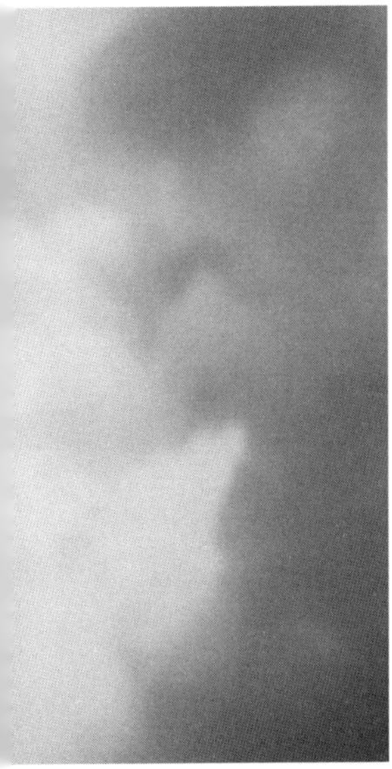

역자의 말

대학에서 학생들을 가르치며 유창한 언변으로 청중들을 사로잡는 일로 늘상
분주한 삶을 살면서도 틈틈이 시를 쓰고 다듬어 아름다운 시집을 탄생시킨
김길연 시인에게 찬사를 보낸다. 이 같은 시인의 열정적인 문학정신을 번역을 통해
되살릴 수 있도록 최선을 다했다. 이러한 노력에 힘을 더해준 번역감수자,
자넬 리브에게 감사를 드린다.

Translator's Remarks

While teaching students at the university and captivating many audiences with
her eloquent speech, the poet took time out of her busy schedule to write poems and polish
them and finally bring out a beautiful poem book.
I praise her for her accomplishment. I did my best to revive her passionate literary spirit
through my translation. I thank my friend and proofreader,
Janell Reeve, who lent weight to my effort.

지 은 이	김길연
개 정 판	2021년 12월 6일
펴 낸 곳	Editorial Design House NAMOO
주　　소	서울시 마포구 서교동 독막로3길 51, 202호
전　　화	02-2268-2592
팩　　스	02-511-2029
홈페이지	www.designnamoo.com
인　　쇄	(주)삼화인쇄
가　　격	15,000원
I S B N	979-11-956548-4-0　03810